25 ESSENTIALS

TECHNIQUES FOR

Wood-Fired Ovens

Every Technique Paired
with a Recipe

A. Cort Sinnes

HARVARD
COMMON
PRESS

Inspiring | Educating | Creating | Entertaining

Brimming with creative inspiration, how-to projects, and useful information to enrich your everyday life, Quarto Knows is a favorite destination for those pursuing their interests and passions. Visit our site and dig deeper with our books into your area of interest: Quarto Creates, Quarto Cooks, Quarto Homes, Quarto Lives, Quarto Drives, Quarto Explores, Quarto Gifts, or Quarto Kids.

© 2018 Quarto Publishing Group USA Inc.

Text © 2018 A. Cort Sinnes

First published in 2018 by The Harvard Common Press, an imprint of The Quarto Group,

100 Cummings Center, Suite 265-D, Beverly, MA 01915, USA.

T (978) 282-9590 F (978) 283-2742 QuartoKnows.com

The Harvard Common Press titles are also available at discount for retail, wholesale, promotional, and bulk purchase. For details, contact the Special Sales Manager by email at specialsales@quarto.com or by mail at The Quarto Group, Attn: Special Sales Manager, 401 Second Avenue North, Suite 310, Minneapolis, MN 55401, USA.

22 21 20 19 18   1 2 3 4 5

ISBN: 978-1-55832-885-3

Digital edition published in 2018

Library of Congress Cataloging-in-Publication Data available

Series design: Traffic Design
Cover Image: Glenn Scott Photography
Page Layout: Megan Jones
Photography: Glenn Scott Photography, unless otherwise noted
Food Styling: Natasha Taylor

Printed in China

Contents

MEATS

VEGETABLES AND SIDES

Introduction:

The Essentials of Cooking in a Wood-Fired Oven

Exactly how long ago our human ancestors started cooking their food is hotly contested (the best estimates are between 400,000 and 1 million years ago), but one thing can be certain: they were using some kind of a live fire to do so.

Things didn't really change much over thousands of years, except for the gradual and comparatively recent move toward containing the fire and being able to control its heat. Ancient Egyptians, Greeks, and Romans all used some type of brick or stone oven, the direct antecedent of today's wood-fired ovens. From the early cast-iron stoves heated by wood fire in the 1700s, the home oven progressed to coal and kerosene (early nineteenth century), gas and electric ovens (early twentieth century), and microwave ovens (mid-twentieth century). And now, with the reemergence of the wood-fired oven, we have come full circle, doubling back on our ancient ancestors. It seems the more digital and abstract we become, the greater our appreciation is for a primitive and primal counterweight. Interestingly, cooking in a wood-fired oven today remains as unpredictable and idiosyncratic as it was a thousand years ago, nothing at all like the precision and consistency we strive for when cooking in any of today's conventional ovens.

Before you get started, be forewarned: there's a fair amount of theater that goes naturally with cooking in a wood-fired oven, even when you're cooking by yourself. If you aren't cooking by yourself, be sure to provide seating for your guests, not only for their comfort but also to keep them out of your way during the heat of the "battle." Folks are drawn to a live fire and will be interested in being part of the process. Without meaning to sound unfriendly, being prepared for this social aspect of wood-fired cooking will help keep you from being derailed by conversation and well-intentioned meddling.

TYPES OF WOOD-FIRED OVENS

Recent years have seen the proliferation of all types of wood-fired ovens, from $149 so-called "pizza ovens," some of which rest on a countertop and others of which stand on legs, to large custom-built masonry ovens that can cost $25,000 and up. Despite their many differences, commercially available wood-fired ovens can be broken down into two categories: black fire and white fire. "Black fire" ovens are those in which the fire is in the same chamber as the food, while the fire in "white fire" ovens is in a separate chamber below the cooking chamber, leaving the latter relatively smoke- and ash-free.

Given their intrinsic idiosyncrasies, it's difficult to make hard-and-fast distinctions between these two types of wood-fired ovens, but for the sake of simplicity, here are a few broad statements that generally hold true:

White fire ovens generally do not achieve the very hot temperatures (in excess of 600°F, or 315°C) associated with black fire ovens. Because it's more difficult to build up residual heat in a white fire oven, it's also more difficult to create conditions where the interior heat of the oven is both relatively hot and sustained over a long period of time—conditions needed, for example, to bake successive loaves of bread. Also, without the presence of a live fire in the cooking chamber, it is more difficult to achieve a crispy exterior on the foods you are cooking. That said, owners of white fire ovens love their ease of use, the speed with which they can be fired up and used for cooking, and their relative cleanliness (no ashes, etcetera, to sweep out of the cooking chamber).

Black fire ovens are the more traditional of the two types of ovens and, frankly, are trickier to use. Black fire ovens heat up and retain their heat differently than white fire ovens. A white fire oven is a little more like a conventional gas or electric oven in that the heat source comes from below and heats the floor of the oven and the interior (the air) space relatively evenly. With a black fire oven, the fire not only heats the air, but it also heats the floor and the ceiling, both of which radiate heat to the food being cooked. If you want your black fire oven to produce relatively even heat over a long period of time, it will need to be heated for several hours, allowing the thermal mass of the oven's floor, walls, and ceiling to thoroughly absorb the heat.

When you first start a fire in a black fire oven, black soot will appear on the inside of the oven's roof. As the oven heats, the soot will turn white and disappear. Once the roof has returned to its original non-soot-covered surface—usually after about an hour—the oven is ready for use. And just for the record, as a general rule, don't add wood to the fire while there's food in the oven. To avoid ash-covered food, if you need to add wood to the fire, remove the food from the oven, add the firewood, and then put the food back.

Unlike the white fire oven, with the fire below the oven floor, if you leave a live fire in the cooking chamber of a black fire oven, you can position the food up next to it to brown and crisp the exterior, revolving it as necessary to achieve an even effect.

You can also rake the coals into an even bed and use what's come to be known as a "Tuscan grill" over the glowing embers for a grilled meal. Or, if you've thoroughly heated the thermal mass of your oven, you can rake out all remnants of the fire and bake enough bread to feed the entire neighborhood. In short, many avid home cooks like the versatility and authenticity of black fire ovens, even though they require somewhat more attention and dedication than white fire ovens.

Please note that the simplicity of the white fire ovens demands nothing more than starting and maintaining a fire in the fire chamber of the oven and adjusting the drafts to achieve the desired temperature of the cooking chamber. Because of this simplicity, and the rapidity with which you will learn to control your white fire oven, the cooking instructions for the recipes in this book—with the exception of recommended cooking temperatures, which are the same for both types of ovens—will pertain solely to black fire ovens.

GENERAL GUIDELINES

The manufacturer of your wood-fired oven will, no doubt, provide you with detailed information regarding all aspects of heating and cooking in your specific oven. The heating of a white fire oven is a straightforward process of starting a fire under the cooking chamber and maintaining it until it has achieved the desired cooking temperature. Heating a black fire oven is a bit more involved. That said, here are a few rules important to remember for both black and white fire ovens:

- Don't use painted or treated wood of any kind, as it may release toxins as the wood is burned. Ditto with any fruit tree prunings that have been sprayed with insecticides. And just to be safe, it's best not to use wood pallets (which seem to be very much in the news these days) unless you know how to read the codes they are stamped with indicating whether they've been simply heat-treated or fumigated with methyl bromide—a substance you're best off avoiding altogether. Because of their high resin content, which causes off-odors in food and excessive smoke, pine logs should also be avoided.

- I've always found a couple of wadded-up sheets of newspaper adequate for starting a fire, but if you're more confident using one of the many fire-starters available commercially, use a brand that is labeled as nontoxic. Never use liquid fuel (fire lighter fluid, gasoline, lantern oil, kerosene, or similar liquids) to start or maintain a fire.

- When it comes time to choose which pan or other cookware to use in your wood-fired oven, don't use anything with wood or plastic handles. Favor stainless-steel pans and terra-cotta cookware—no glass, or Teflon, or similarly nonstick coated pans. Cast-iron frying pans and Dutch ovens can definitely be used, but considering that cast iron doesn't melt until it reaches somewhere around 2,100°F (1,150°C), these pans can actually get too hot when the oven temperature is extreme—so be forewarned. Round pans are great (like a paella pan), as they tend to be easy to spin, making it simple to brown or crisp food on all sides. My favorite cookware for the wood-fired oven is the combination of a metal cooling rack and a metal baking sheet with short sides. With a little effort, you can find a cooling rack and baking sheet that more or less match in size; even better is a round cooling rack that fits inside a round pan, like a cake pan. Keeping the food off the surface of the pan allows the hot, wood-fired air to completely surround what's being cooked, producing a nice, even degree of doneness. A friend of mine who is a longtime wood-fired-oven cook agrees completely regarding the efficiency of using a raised metal rack but stopped using the pan under the rack years ago, saying, "Why clean the pan when the oven floor cleans itself?"

COOKING TEMPERATURE AND TIMES

It helps to remind yourself that wood-fired oven cooking is not a precise endeavor and a somewhat relaxed attitude is all but necessary if you're going to enjoy the process. This is especially true of temperatures and cooking times. But wait a minute, you might say—aren't those two of the most important components of being a successful cook? Yes and no. If you can control them, by all means do, but if precise control is out of the question, learn to roll with the punches. Which brings us to another point: wood-fired cooking demands close attention. It's not the kind of endeavor that allows the practitioner to wander off to pull a few weeds or talk to the neighbor over the back fence. Every wood-fired oven is a little different, and the way that you become familiar with its idiosyncrasies and learn to adapt to them is by paying attention. Knowing how to confidently use your wood-fired oven is what makes it a pleasurable activity.

Almost every manufacturer of wood-fired ovens cannot resist the temptation to put a thermometer in the oven door. At best, they are in a precarious location, seemingly destined to fail somewhere down the road. The good news is that by the time the built-in thermometer fails, you'll be determining the temperature of the oven using all kinds of other clues and indicators based on your unique experience with the oven and you won't miss the oven door thermometer. That said, you'll still want to have two different thermometers on hand—an instant-read one and an infrared one. See "Accessories" on page 18.

Your wood-fired oven is going to come with a great deal of detailed information on building and maintaining a fire. By all means, read the manufacturer's instructions carefully; they know what they're talking about and it's in their best interest to provide specific information to make you a success as a wood-fired chef. Without going into the specifics of your individual oven, here's an overview of the fire-making and heating process.

You're going to start by building a fire toward the opening of the oven, using dry hardwood, probably 10 inches (25.5 cm) or so in length and in an assortment of diameters, from big (about 4 inches, or 10 cm, in diameter) to smaller, kindling-size wood (1 inch, or 2.5 cm, or less in diameter). Start the stack with a couple of bigger pieces and then continue building with smaller pieces, as if you were playing Jenga; leave enough room for a crumpled piece of newspaper or two at the base of the stack. Light the paper and let the fire catch. Once it's burning well, push the fire to the center of the oven. Let it burn for about an hour, leaving the door open, adding more pieces of smallish wood as needed. As the oven heats, you'll notice black soot forming on the oven's ceiling and, as it gets hotter, the soot burning off, or "clearing," as it is called. At this point, using the metal peel, shovel, or "poker," push the fire to the back or side of the oven, opening up space for cooking. Use the metal brush to sweep the ashes from the floor. The clearing process will probably take about an hour and is the signal that the oven is ready for cooking. The oven will probably be in the 700°F (370°C) range, just right for pizza or other thin flatbreads, which cook in an instant. Leave the door open to allow the temperature of the oven to diminish slightly; keep the door almost closed to keep the temperature more constant. The longer the oven is heated, the longer it will slowly release the accumulated heat and, hence, the longer the amount of time you have to cook.

ACCESSORIES

As this is the most primitive of all cooking methods, it's fitting that one can get by with the bare minimum of tools and equipment. Here's the short list:

- **Fireplace lighter with a long "snout."** You'll need the extra length to reach into the oven to easily light the fire.

- **Two thermometers:** A "point-and-shoot" infrared thermometer for reading the temperature of any surface in the oven interior and an instant-read thermometer with a probe for testing the "doneness" of any food. In essence, you need the infrared thermometer to help determine when to put the food in the oven and the instant-read thermometer to advise you as to when to take it out.

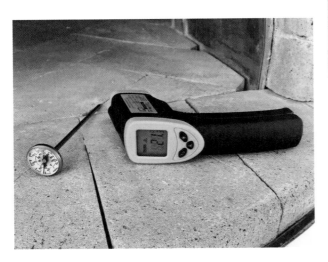

- **Heat-resistant gloves**, especially those with extra-long gauntlet cuffs that cover your forearms. This is one item you don't want to scrimp on, so buy the best pair you can. Do not put unprotected hands or arms inside the oven while it is lit.

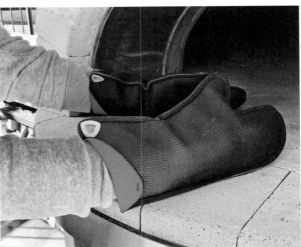

- **Two peels, metal and wood:** The wooden one for baking (less likely to damage the dough than a metal peel) and the metal peel for everything from moving burning logs to repositioning pots and pans in the oven to, of course, getting pizzas out when done.

- **Brush with metal bristles** for brushing out hot ashes.
- **Metal fireplace shovel** with a fairly long handle for all manner of fire maintenance, including shoveling out ashes and spent coals.

- **Small metal trash can with lid for ashes.** Live coals—even small ones—can remain hot and dangerous much longer than you might imagine. It's always best to store them in a nonflammable metal container until the ashes and coals have gone cold.
- **Roll of heavy-duty aluminum foil** for shielding food from too much heat, "tenting" food while it rests after coming out of the oven, wrapping leftovers, and all manner of other needs.
- **Some kind of a long-handled, metal utensil**— similar to a fireplace poker—for all-purpose use. It doesn't really have a name, but whatever you call it, it will come in very handy for managing the fire, pushing hot pots and pans around the oven, and pulling them out.

SAFETY

- Keep children and pets away from the hot oven.

- Be aware that flying sparks can escape from the opening of the oven. Ensure that no combustible materials are within range of the oven at any time.

- Don't close the oven door completely while a fire is in the oven. Closing the door fully will cut off oxygen to the fire, causing the fire to reignite suddenly when the door is opened. Always keep the door slightly ajar to allow air to circulate in the oven.

- Do not use water to dampen or extinguish fire in the oven. Always keep a functioning 5-pound model Class A fire extinguisher close at hand.

- Fire can result from incorrect installation or use of the oven. It is essential to use only building and insulation materials designed for the purpose.

- Contact your local building department for clarification on any restrictions on installation of this oven in your area.

Makes 2 large or 4 smaller pizzas

Pizza 101

Somewhere along the way to their increased popularity, wood-fired ovens began to be called "pizza ovens," owing to the fact that pizza was what most people cooked in them. Enthusiasts have always known that anything that can be cooked in a regular oven can be cooked in a wood-fired oven—only everything turns out better coming from a wood-fired oven. I'm not going to disagree as to their versatility, but I know one thing for sure: if you want to bring a smile to virtually anyone's face—young, old, and in between—offer them a pizza hot from your wood-fired oven. If there were such a thing as a "culinary hero," part of the hero's journey would definitely include learning to make these pizzas!

INGREDIENTS

(for the dough)

1 package active dry yeast

1 teaspoon kosher salt

1 tablespoon (15 ml) olive oil

1 cup (235 ml) warm (100°F to 110°F, or 38°C to 43°C) water

About 4 cups (500 g) unsifted unbleached all-purpose flour

Cornmeal or semolina flour, for the pizza peel

METHOD

1. Preheat your wood-fired oven for about 45 minutes before cooking. You want it to be good and hot when ready to cook: 650°F to 750°F (345°C to 400°C).

2. Add the yeast, salt, and olive oil to the warm water in a large bowl. Mix until smooth.

3. Gradually add the flour, starting with 3½ cups (438 g).

4. Knead the dough. If you're using your hands, turn the dough onto a board coated with the remaining ½ cup (62 g) flour and knead until smooth and elastic, about 5 minutes. If you're using a mixer, blend the dough on low speed with the dough hook and then mix on medium speed until the dough is smooth and elastic, 7 to 10 minutes. Expect the dough to still feel a little tacky.

5. Place the dough in a lightly greased bowl, cover it with a clean kitchen towel, and letit rise in a warm, draft-free place for 1 to 1½ hours, until it has doubled in size.

6. Punch down the dough and let it rise again until doubled, 30 to 40 minutes. After it has doubled, knead it on a lightly floured board and shape into a smooth ball. Divide the dough in half and roll out each portion on the floured board until it is about ¾ inch (2 cm) thick. Gently pull each portion into an oval 12 to 14 inches (30 to 36 cm) long and 8 to 10 inches (20 to 25.5 cm) wide. If you want four smaller, round pizzas, by all means simply divide the dough into four equal parts. Place on a floured board and roll into 8- to 10-inch (20 to 25.5 cm) circles. A typical thin-crust pizza starts out with dough between ¾ and ¼ inch (2 cm and 6 mm) thick. Common sense dictates that the thinner the dough, the trickier it will be to work with and the fewer toppings it will be able to support.

7. Once the dough is stretched to the size you want, gently slide the pieces, working with one at a time, onto a wooden peel that has been dusted with a combination of flour and cornmeal or semolina flour. Once the crust is on the peel, it's time to add the toppings.

8. Regarding toppings: the basic rule is not to overdo it. Too much in the topping department makes for a soggy pizza. A second rule is the better quality the toppings, the better the pizza. As far as the tomato sauce goes, spoon it on sparingly, spreading it out in a circular motion, keeping it about ½ inch (1.2 cm) from the edge. After the tomato sauce, add your favorite toppings (see page 28), remembering that less is more.

9. Check the oven. Position the remnants of the fire to one side or the other. Use your oven brush to clean the floor, and wait 10 minutes or so for the temperature to settle. When it comes time to put the pizza in the oven, it pays to be decisive. Hold the handle of the peel with both hands and, using a back-and-forth movement, slide the pizza from the peel, landing it in the center of the oven floor.

10. Cook the pizza for 1½ to 2 minutes. Switch to the metal peel and rotate the pizza 180 degrees. Continue cooking for another 1½ to 2 minutes, until the edges of the pizza crust start to brown.

11. Using the metal peel, remove the pizza from the oven. Allow it to rest for a couple of minutes on a wire rack, which will permit some of the steam to escape and keep the crust from getting soggy before cutting.

Makes 2 large calzones

Calzone

Calzone is a folded-over cousin to the pizza. As such, when you roll the dough, you'll need to keep it a little thicker (about ¼ inch, or 6 mm, thick) so it is sturdy enough to hold its precious filling safely inside. Because they are completely covered with dough, any calzone filling should be cooked prior to being used, otherwise you'll wind up with a crispy crust enclosing a combination of raw fillings.

INGREDIENTS

(for the dough)

1 batch Pizza 101 dough (page 22)

(suggestions for the toppings)

¼ cup (60 g) tomato sauce

1 cup (115 g) shredded cheese

Olives

Artichoke hearts

Mushrooms

Caramelized onions

Fennel

Pineapple

Pesto

Pepperoni

Salami

Sausage

Bacon

Canadian bacon

Diced chicken

METHOD

1. Preheat your wood-fired oven for about 45 minutes before cooking. You want it to be very hot when ready to cook: about 600°F (315°C).

2. Prepare the dough recipe given for pizza on page 22.

3. After the dough has doubled the second time, knead it on a board dusted with all-purpose flour or semolina flour. Divide the dough in half and roll out each portion on the floured board until it is about 10 inches (25.5 cm) in diameter and ¼ inch (6 mm) thick.

4. Fillings for calzone are basically the same as for pizza, with the exception that anything that needs cooking, such as spinach, bacon, or raw sausage, needs to be cooked before use as a calzone filling.

5. Arrange the fillings (including tomato sauce, if desired) over one-half of each dough round.

6. Fold the exposed part of the dough round over the ingredients, pinching to close the edges, like you would do with a fruit pie.

7. Check the oven. Push the remnants of the fire to one side of the oven or the other. Use your oven brush to clean the floor and wait 10 minutes or so for the temperature to settle.

8. Transfer the calzone to a wooden pizza peel that has been generously dusted with all-purpose flour or semolina flour. Using a back-and-forth movement, slide the calzone from the peel, placing it in the center of the oven floor. Cook until the dough puffs and turns golden on top, 8 to 10 minutes. If you have a black fire oven, keep the oven door almost completely closed while the calzone are cooking.

9. Switch to a metal peel and remove the calzone from the oven. Allow to rest on a wire rack for a couple of minutes before serving. Serve hot.

Makes 1 large pizza bianca

Pizza Bianca

This wonderful recipe was developed by J. Kenji López-Alt, the managing culinary director of the culinary website Serious Eats; I adapted the baking instructions, with Kenji's kind permission, to work with the wood-fired oven. Kenji has some serious credentials, including writing *The Food Lab: Better Home Cooking Through Science*, which was not only a *New York Times* best seller but also a winner of both a James Beard Award and named Cookbook of the Year in 2015 by the International Association of Culinary Professionals.

If you've never had pizza bianca, you're in for a real treat. Here's how Kenji describes it: "At first glance, pizza bianca looks pretty similar to certain types of focaccia, the olive oil–laden Italian bread, but the similarities are mostly superficial. Focaccia is made with an enriched dough—it has oil in it—which gives it a moister, softer texture with far less chew than pizza bianca, which is made with a lean dough. While focaccia is baked in a pan, pizza bianca is baked directly on the floor of the oven, much like a Neapolitan pizza." The flavor and texture of pizza bianca are heaven-sent: crispy on the outside, chewy on the inside. Learn to make this and become a star chef—no kidding.

INGREDIENTS

3¼ cups (406 g) bread flour

2 teaspoons kosher salt

1½ teaspoons instant or rapid-rise yeast

1 cup plus 10½ tablespoons lukewarm water (13.25 ounces, or 395 ml)

¼ cup (60 ml) extra-virgin olive oil

Coarse sea salt

1 tablespoon (1.7 g) finely chopped fresh rosemary leaves (optional)

METHOD

1. Combine the flour, kosher salt, and yeast in a large bowl and whisk together until homogenous. Add the lukewarm water and stir with a wooden spoon until no dry flour remains. Cover the bowl tightly with plastic wrap and allow to rest at room temperature overnight.

2. The next day, lightly flour the dough and your hands. Scrape the dough out of the bowl onto a well-floured piece of parchment paper set inside a rimmed baking sheet and gently fold the dough into an even blob in the center. Dust with flour and cover with a clean kitchen towel. Allow to rise at room temperature until nearly doubled in volume, about 2 hours.

3. Meanwhile, preheat your wood-fired oven for about 45 minutes before cooking. You want it to be hot when ready to cook: about 550°F (290°C).

4. About 30 minutes before baking, check the oven temperature. Gently stretch the dough into an even rectangular shape to fit the baking sheet (you shouldn't have to lift it). Carefully stipple the top surface with your fingertips. Drizzle with the olive oil and sprinkle with the sea salt and rosemary, if using. Push the remnants of the fire to one side of the oven or the other. Use your oven brush to clean the floor and wait 10 minutes or so for the temperature to settle. Transfer the entire baking sheet with the dough to the middle of the wood-fired oven. Close the door almost completely.

5. Bake for 5 minutes, just until the pizza is slightly firm. Remove from the oven and transfer the pizza to a pizza peel. Discard the parchment paper. Return the pizza to bake directly on the floor of the oven until burnished golden brown, 10 to 15 minutes longer. Remove from the oven and allow to cool for 5 minutes on a wire rack. Transfer to a large cutting board, cut into 8 or 12 rectangular slices, and serve.

Makes 8 large pretzels

Pretzels

Just for ducks, I looked up "flatbread" on Wikipedia and there are 104 entries, everything from Native American fry bread to naan to green onion pancakes from China, Norwegian lefse, Ugandan chapati, and on and on—and I don't think they listed them all. So why not pretzels? They qualify as a flatbread and definitely earn you kudos as a cook while folks are standing around the wood-fired oven, glass in hand, waiting for the main event. This recipe was developed by the King Arthur Flour folks, who know a thing or two about all things baked. It's a winner.

INGREDIENTS

(for the dough)

2½ cups (313 g) unbleached all-purpose flour

2¼ teaspoons instant or rapid-rise yeast

1 teaspoon salt

1 teaspoon sugar

⅞ to 1 cup (220 to 235 ml) warm water*

Use the greater amount in the winter, the lesser amount in the summer, and somewhere in between in the spring and fall. Your goal is a soft dough.

(for the topping)

1 cup (235 ml) water, boiling

2 tablespoons (27.5 g) baking soda

3 tablespoons (42 g) unsalted butter, melted

Coarse kosher salt

METHOD

1. Preheat your wood-fired oven about an hour before cooking. You want it to be hot when ready to cook: about 475°F (240°C).

2. To make the dough by hand, or with a mixer: Place all of the dough ingredients into a bowl, and beat until well combined. Knead the dough, by hand or mixer, for about 5 minutes, until it's soft, smooth, and quite slack. Dust the dough with flour, place it in a bag, and allow it to rest for 30 minutes.

3. To make the dough with a bread machine: Place all of the dough ingredients into the pan of your bread machine, program the machine for Dough or Manual, and press Start. Allow the dough to proceed through its kneading cycle (no need to let it rise), then cancel the machine, dust the dough with flour, and give it a rest in a plastic bag as instructed in step 1.

4. To make the dough with a food processor: Place the flour, yeast, salt, and sugar in the work bowl of a food processor equipped with the steel blade. Process for 5 seconds. Add the water, and process for 7 to 10 seconds, until the dough starts to clear the sides of the bowl. Process for another 45 seconds. Place a handful of flour in a bowl, scoop the slack dough into the bowl, and shape the dough into a ball, coating it with the flour. Transfer the dough to a plastic bag, close the bag loosely, leaving room for the dough to expand, and let it rest at room temperature for 30 minutes.

5. While the dough is resting, prepare the topping: Combine the boiling water and baking soda, stirring until the soda is totally (or almost totally) dissolved. Set the mixture aside to cool to lukewarm (or cooler).

6. Check your oven temperature. If it's cooler than 475°F (240°C), add a little wood to the fire; you want enough built-up heat to sustain an hour's worth of cooking. Cut 8 pieces of parchment paper to about 7 by 10 inches (17.5 by 25.5 cm). Set aside.

7. Transfer the dough to a lightly greased work surface, and divide it into 8 equal pieces (about 2½ ounces, or 70 g, each). Allow the pieces to rest, uncovered, for 5 minutes. Pour the baking soda–water mixture into a 9-inch (23 cm) square pan.

8. Roll each piece of dough into a long, thin rope (28 to 30 inches, or 70 to 75 cm long), and twist each rope into a pretzel shape. Working with 4 pretzels at a time, place them in the pan with the baking soda–water mixture, spooning the water over their tops; leave them in the water for 2 minutes before placing them on a baking sheet. This baking soda "bath" will give the pretzels a nice golden brown color after cooking.

9. Put one pretzel on each of the pieces of parchment paper. Using a pizza peel, slide the pretzels on their parchment pieces to within 8 inches (20 cm) of the coals inside the oven. Close the door completely. Bake for 7 minutes; the pretzels will almost double in height. After 7 minutes, carefully turn the parchment, using a metal peel and a gloved hand, and bake for another 7 to 8 minutes, again with the door closed.

10. Remove the pretzels from the oven when they are golden brown, and brush them thoroughly with the melted butter. Keep brushing the butter on until you've used it all up; it may seem like a lot, but that's what gives these pretzels their ethereal taste. Sprinkle them lightly with salt. Allow them to rest, uncovered, for at least 10 minutes. These are best served warm; they can be reheated in the oven.

5 | BREAD BAKING IN A WOOD-FIRED OVEN

Makes 3 large loaves, or more smaller ones

A Basic Loaf Bread

When you start experimenting with baking bread in a wood-fired oven, you've entered some pretty rarified culinary territory—territory that's engaging and fun, not to mention delicious and deeply satisfying on some primal level. There is more than one book devoted solely to the subject of wood-fired baking, so all I can do here on these few pages is provide an introduction to the subject with the most basic of loaves. For a lucky few, it will be enough to get them started on a very long and enjoyable journey.

INGREDIENTS

1 package (2¼ teaspoons or 7 g) active dry yeast

4 teaspoons sugar

4 cups (950 ml) warm water (between 100°F and 110°F, or 38°C to 43°C)

11 to 12 cups (1.4 to 1.5 kg) unsifted unbleached all-purpose flour

1 tablespoon (18 g) kosher salt

Vegetable oil

1 egg, beaten well with ¼ cup (60 ml) water

Water (and a spray bottle for spraying the bread in the oven)

METHOD

1. Stir the yeast and sugar into the warm water in a large bowl. Using your fingers, mix the ingredients until the yeast is dissolved. Using a heavy wooden spoon, stir in 10 cups (1.3 kg) of the flour and the salt and mix well to form a sticky dough.

2. Turn the dough out onto a board coated with 1 cup (125 g) of the flour. To make it easier to handle, sprinkle some of the flour over the dough and then knead for about 10 minutes, or until the dough is smooth; add more flour, if necessary.

3. Oil a large bowl generously with vegetable oil; place the dough in the bowl and cover the bowl with plastic wrap. Set the bowl in a warm, draft-free place and let the dough rise for 1 hour 15 minutes, or until doubled in size.

4. Meanwhile, preheat your wood-fired oven. You want it to get good and hot and then cool to be at about 350°F (180°C) by the time you're ready to cook.

5. Once you've started the fire in the oven, take the risen dough and divide it into equal portions, depending on the size of loaf you want—anything from 2 to 8 portions. Shape each portion into a ball and then form the ball into the shape you want, be it oval, round, or a long, baguette-like loaf.

6. Cover a couple of baking sheets with muslin cloth (like a flour sack cloth) and dust with flour. Leaving space in between them, place the loaves on the floured cloths and then cover with cotton cloths. Allow to rise at room temperature for 30 to 40 minutes.

7. After the oven has burned for an hour or so, use your oven brush to clean the floor of embers and ashes. Close the oven door completely.

8. When the oven has cooled to about 350°F (180°C), prepare to place the loaves in the oven. Dust a wooden peel with flour and have it at the ready. Lift the edge of the bottom cloth to roll a loaf slightly onto the palm of your hand and then slip the peel under the loaf and roll the loaf onto the peel using your hand. Make shallow, diagonal cuts across the top of the loaf using a very sharp knife. Brush the top of the loaf with the beaten egg mixture.

9. Open the oven door. Using a back-and-forth movement, slide the loaf from the peel, placing it on the oven floor. Repeat this process with the remaining loaves. When they are all in place, close the door. After 10 minutes, spray the loaves all over with water. Close the door and bake for another 10 minutes, and then spray the loaves with water again.

10. Close the door and continue baking for another 40 to 60 minutes, depending on the size of your loaves and the oven temperature, until the bread is a rich, golden brown. Once you suspect your loaf is done, turn it upside down (wearing a heat-resistant glove) and tap the bottom with your fingernail. The loaf is done if the sound is hollow. Use a metal peel to remove the loaves from the oven. Let cool on wire racks before you slice.

Serves 4

Side of Salmon

Here's a dish that comes together quickly and easily, certain to advance your reputation as a talented cook. Start with a side of salmon with the skin on, figuring about a ½-pound (225 g) per person for normal appetites. Over the years, I've gravitated toward using high heat and fast cooking for fish, and the wood-fired oven is perfect for this—with the added benefit that it doesn't cause the smoke detector to go off, as has happened a few times when I've used this method indoors.

Salmon can stand up to all manner of assertive flavor combos. One of the favorites around here is to serve it with red Thai curry sauce with a scattering of blanched snow peas and steamed sticky rice, or on a pool of black bean purée with a drizzle of red pepper purée and fresh lime juice squeezed over the top. In a pinch, a couple of fresh lemons and some snipped fresh dill will work wonders. You get the idea. To make it easier to serve after it's cooked, score the raw salmon across the fillet with cuts about ¼ inch (6 mm) deep, the size of individual servings.

INGREDIENTS

4 salmon fillets, about 8 ounces (225 g) each

Olive oil

Kosher salt and freshly ground pepper

METHOD

1. In an indoor oven, I cook this at 450°F (230°C), so let that be your guide as you preheat your wood-fired oven.

2. Arrange the salmon on a rimmed baking sheet, drizzle with olive oil, and flip the fillet over a couple of times to thoroughly coat it with the oil. With the skin-side down, sprinkle the salmon with salt and pepper.

3. Place in the oven and cook for 12 minutes, at which point the salmon should be cooked perfectly. The salmon is done when the thickest portion is opaque at the center. You can check by turning a fork gently in the salmon. It's that simple. Serve with the sauce of your choice, or simply a couple of lemon wedges.

Serves 6

Swordfish Fillets Wrapped in Prosciutto

Swordfish is a dense, meaty fish with a mild flavor, excellent for standing up to the rustic qualities of a wood-fired oven. Wrapping the swordfish steaks with thin slices of prosciutto takes the fish to another level of deliciousness. Whether you're using previously frozen or fresh swordfish, make sure you pat it very dry before rubbing with olive oil—this is especially true for previously frozen fish. Nothing more than a wedge or two of fresh lemon is needed to complement this dish.

INGREDIENTS

6 swordfish steaks, about 8 ounces (225 g) each, 1 inch (2.5 cm) thick

Olive oil

6 thin slices prosciutto

Lemon wedges

METHOD

1. Preheat your wood-fired oven. You want it to be at about 450°F (230°C) when ready to cook.

2. Start by rinsing the swordfish steaks and thoroughly drying them. Rub lightly with olive oil and then wrap each steak with a single slice of prosciutto. Prosciutto naturally sticks to itself, so as long as you overlap it, the prosciutto will stay in place during the cooking process.

3. I prefer using a rack placed in a shallow pan for the swordfish, as you won't have to turn the fish, but a heavy metal skillet works as well. If you use the rack-and-pan method, the steaks will cook in about 10 minutes in the preheated oven. If you opt for cooking them in a metal pan, cook at the same temperature for 5 minutes and then turn the swordfish steaks and cook for another 4 to 5 minutes. Serve immediately, with lemon wedges.

Serves 4 to 6

Chicken Thighs, Legs, and Wings

I may be putting too fine a point on it, but I think chicken dark meat—the wings, legs, and thighs— is better suited to the wood-fired oven than chicken breast meat. Or maybe I just like the dark meat better? Whatever you choose, go with chicken that's raised as close to your home as possible, by a farmer using the most natural husbandry methods as practical. There's a big difference in taste, no doubt about it. If you've gone to the effort to procure a tasty, local chicken, I say keep it simple and let those natural flavors shine through. Over the years, I gradually gravitated toward brining chicken in a simple brine and then roasting it with a little olive oil and some complementary combination of dried herbs; you can't go wrong with herbes de Provence, a classic French combination of basil, savory, thyme, marjoram, and rosemary, or try the Napa Valley Rub from Whole Spice (http://wholespice.com). It's a unique combination of sun-dried tomatoes, rosemary, lemon peel, fennel seed, black pepper, chile, garlic, citric acid, and sea salt and has become my go-to herb blend for all kinds of poultry.

INGREDIENTS

6 cups (1.4 L) cold water

¾ cup (216 g) kosher salt

¾ cup (150 g) sugar

5 pounds (2.3 kg) chicken thighs, legs, and wings (about 5 each)

Olive oil

Dried herb blend of your choice

METHOD

1. Mix the water, salt, and sugar in a 1-gallon (3.8 l) resealable plastic bag until the salt and sugar are dissolved. Add the chicken parts and allow to brine in the refrigerator for 2 hours.

2. Meanwhile, preheat your wood-fired oven. You want it to be at about 400°F (200°C) when ready to cook.

3. Remove the chicken from the brine and pat thoroughly dry. Coat the chicken parts with olive oil and liberally sprinkle with the herb blend.

4. I prefer using a rack placed in a shallow pan for the chicken, but a large, heavy metal skillet works as well. If you use the rack-and-pan method, the chicken will cook in 40 to 50 minutes in the preheated oven. For even browning, turn once or twice during the roasting process. If you opt for cooking the chicken in a metal pan, cook at the same temperature for the same time, turning the chicken every 10 minutes or so. This chicken is delicious hot, cold, or at room temperature.

Serves 5 or 6

Whole Roasted Butterflied Turkey

It's kind of a shame that turkey has become so completely associated with Thanksgiving in this country that we rarely think about at other times of the year. Turkeys are tasty birds and an economical way to serve a crowd, especially when you leave those traditional holiday accompaniments behind and embrace a different approach—say, Mexican. The flavors of Mexico combine nicely with turkey, and your finished dish will be right at home folded in a warm tortilla, topped with some fresh lime juice and chopped cilantro. Good eating!

INGREDIENTS

One turkey, 10 to 12 pounds (4.6 to 5.5 kg)

¾ cup (175 ml) neutral vegetable oil, plus more for drizzling

¾ cup (175 ml) unsweetened pineapple juice

½ cup (120 ml) fresh lime juice

2 teaspoons chili powder (hot or mild)

2 teaspoons dried oregano, crumbled

1 teaspoon kosher salt

Corn or flour tortillas, warmed on the floor of the wood-fired oven

Lime wedges

Chopped fresh cilantro (optional)

METHOD

1. Flatten the turkey by placing it on a sturdy surface, breast-side up. With a heavy chef's knife, cleaver, or pair of poultry shears, cut through the ribs on one side, as close to the backbone as possible. Make a second cut on the other side of the backbone, again as close to the backbone as possible. Remove the backbone completely.

2. Turn the bird breast-side down and spread the rib cage apart. If you make a notch in the end of the breastbone near the wishbone, it will be easier to spread the rib cage.

3. Turn the bird over and flatten with the heel of your hand. Expect some of the rib bones to break.

4. Fold the wing tips under the wings, make a slit in the bird's skin near the edge of each breast, and tuck in the legs for a neat "package," ready for marinating and roasting.

5. Combine the oil, juices, chili powder, oregano, and salt in a 2-gallon (7.6 L) resealable plastic bag. Place the turkey in the bag, seal it, and turn the bag a few times to coat the turkey with the marinade. Let marinade in the refrigerator for 4 to 6 hours or, preferably, overnight.

6. When ready to cook, preheat your wood-fired oven to between 400°F and 500°F (200°C and 250°C).

7. Remove the turkey from the marinade and place on a rimmed baking sheet. Pat dry and then drizzle with a light coating of vegetable oil.

8. You are going to want to roast the turkey until an instant-read meat thermometer stuck into the thickest part of the breast registers 170°F (77°C), which, in a moderate oven, will take between 90 minutes and 2 hours. If your oven is any hotter than 500°F (250°C), you'll probably need to wrap the turkey loosely in aluminum foil to keep it from burning during the initial 30 minutes or so of cooking. You can remove the foil as the oven cools. However, if your oven is less than 400°F (200°C) at the start of cooking, it is probably best to start a small fire to help keep the temperature consistent over the relatively long cooking time. If you build a small fire, you'll need to rotate the turkey a couple of times to help it cook and brown evenly.

9. Once the turkey has reached 170°F (77°C), remove it from the oven, tent loosely with foil, and allow to rest for 10 to 15 minutes. To carve the turkey, start on one side or the other. Cut the leg and thigh sections completely off, then do the same with the wings. Slice the breast meat off in thin slices, then cut the meat from the legs, thighs, and wings. Repeat on the other side. Serve with warmed tortillas, lime wedges, and cilantro, if desired.

1 or 2 quail per person

Quail, Butterflied or Not

I'm a big fan of quail, and the high heat of a wood-fired oven is very well suited to the quick roasting of these tiny birds. I don't think it's necessary to add much to the delicious flavor of quail, so I don't brine them, preferring to simply butterfly them, rub them with a little olive oil and dust with salt and freshly ground pepper, and roast them on a rack-and-pan combination. To butterfly, place the quail breast-side up on a cutting board. Insert a sharp butcher's knife into the cavity and cut on both sides of the backbone to remove it completely. You can also roast quail whole, but you may find them a little difficult to keep upright. Either butterflied or whole, rinse the quail in cold water and pat dry before rubbing with olive oil and salt and pepper. Serve with just a couple of wedges of fresh lemon, some polenta or risotto (page 110), and a fresh vegetable, and you're in for some world-class dining.

INGREDIENTS

1 or 2 quail per person

Olive oil

Salt and freshly ground black pepper

Lemon wedges (optional)

METHOD

1. Preheat your wood-fired oven to between 450°F and 600°F (230°C and 315°C), depending on how you are cooking them (see step 3).

2. If desired, butterfly the quail, using the method described in the headnote. Whether whole or butterflied, rinse the quail in cold water and thoroughly pat dry. Rub all sides generously with olive oil and dust with salt and pepper.

3. I prefer roasting the butterflied quail on a rack placed in a shallow pan. If you opt for this method, the quail can be roasted at about 600°F (315°C) for about 5 minutes or so and then loosely tented with aluminum foil for 5 to 10 minutes. If you leave the birds whole and roast them in a metal pan, leave some room between them so the heat can circulate and cook at a lower temperature—in the 450°F (230°C) range—for 12 to 18 minutes. Loosely tent with foil and allow to rest for 5 to 10 minutes before serving with lemon wedges, if desired.

Serves 6 to 8

"Peking" Duck Breast

The origins of this recipe go back thirty-plus years to when a friend of mine ordered Peking duck at the famous Mr. Chow's restaurant in Beverly Hills and called it a "duck burrito." Purists may dismiss this take on the famous dish, but non-purists will probably be coming back for thirds. I substituted flour tortillas (the thinnest ones I could find) for the Chinese pancakes traditionally called for and, instead of composing a sauce, I simply used store-bought hoisin sauce. The combination of hoisin sauce, scallions, and cucumbers along with the marinated duck breast slices wrapped up in a warm flour tortilla makes for some pretty fine eating.

INGREDIENTS

6 duck breast halves

6 tablespoons (120 g) honey

¼ cup (60 ml) dry white wine

2 tablespoons (28 ml) soy sauce

¼ cup (25 g) Chinese five-spice powder

Salt and freshly ground pepper (white preferred)

1 package flour tortillas, the thinnest you can find

1 jar store-bought hoisin sauce

1 bunch scallions, cut into matchstick slices

1 cucumber, peeled,

seeded, and cut into matchstick slices

METHOD

1. Using a sharp knife, score the duck skin about ⅛ inch (3 mm) deep in a crisscross pattern.

2. Combine the honey, wine, soy sauce, Chinese five-spice, salt, and pepper in a 1-gallon (3.8 L) resealable plastic bag and massage the bag until the ingredients are combined. Add the duck breast halves to the plastic bag and allow to marinate in the refrigerator for 2 hours, or as long as overnight.

3. Preheat your wood-fired oven to about 450°F (230°C).

4. Pat the duck breasts dry. I prefer to cook them on a rack set in a pan, skin-side up. By doing so, you don't need to flip them. They can also be cooked in a cast-iron pan, starting with them skin-side down for 3 to 4 minutes and then turning them and cooking for another 2 to 3 minutes. Duck breasts are just small enough to make it difficult to use an instant-read thermometer; better is to learn to read their doneness by pressing on them with your finger. If they feel about as soft/springy as your cheek, they're rare. If they feel more like your chin, they're medium, and if they feel like your forehead, they're well-done. No matter how you like them cooked, tent them loosely with aluminum foil for about 10 minutes before slicing.

5. Cut the flour tortillas in half and briefly warm them directly on the floor of the wood-fired oven. Lay down a stripe of hoisin sauce on each tortilla, add the duck slices, top with some scallion and cucumber strips, and fold the tortilla over. Good eating!

Florentine Steak

If you're lucky enough to have access to a wood-fired oven, this traditional favorite from Florence, Italy, is a pretty straightforward proposition. The first step is to ask your friendly butcher to cut you the best T-bone steaks, 2 inches (5 cm) thick. The steaks should be well aged and marbled. I'm of the opinion that you need a rack-and-pan combination to prepare this steak properly. Other methods I've seen recommended (such as the use of a Tuscan grill over a bed of coals or placing the steak in a wire basket and placing the basket directly on the coals) result in a steak bathed in smoke from fat dripping onto coals. Not only has this been determined to be unhealthy, but Gerbase Markham, a cookbook author from the middle 1600s, wrote, "the smoak [sic] occasioned by the droppings of the meat will ascend about it and make a stink." The rack-and-pan method will completely avoid the occasion of any "stink." For the record, the Florentines pretty much only prepare this steak one way: charred on the outside and rare in the middle. One T-bone steak cut this way will feed two people, probably with leftovers—or not.

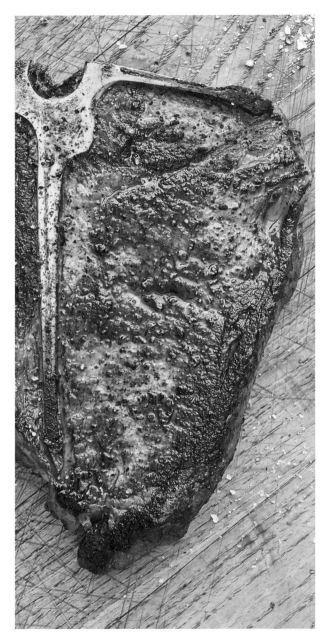

INGREDIENTS

T-bone steak (1½ pounds, 680g), well marbled and aged, cut 2 inches (5 cm) thick

Olive oil

Kosher salt and freshly ground black pepper

METHOD

1. Preheat your wood-fired oven to between 450°F and 500°F (230°C and 250°C).

2. Allow the steaks to come to room temperature. Rub liberally with olive oil and dust with salt and pepper.

3. Place the steak on a wire rack set over a pan. Place the pan next to the fire in the oven. Close the door almost completely and let the steak cook for 15 minutes, at which point the steak will be nicely browned on the outside and rare inside.

4. Remove the pan from the oven and loosely tent with aluminum foil for 5 minutes or so. Slice and serve immediately.

Serves 8 to 10

Wagon Train Chuck Pot Roast and Beans

This is an old-fashioned, hearty combination perfect for a hungry crowd of 8 to 10 eaters. Make sure your Dutch oven can accommodate a 6-pound (2.7 kg) cut of beef and a pound (455 g) of beans before you embark on this dish. Unless your oven has been very well heated over a relatively long time, to maintain a 350°F (180°C) temperature for approximately 3 hours, you may need to judiciously stoke the fire during the cooking process.

INGREDIENTS

1 pound (455 g) dried pinto beans, rinsed and picked over

1 tablespoon (15 ml) vegetable oil

1 bottom round beef roast, 6 pounds (2.7 kg)

2 cups (475 ml) tomato juice

1 can (8 ounces, or 235 ml) tomato sauce

½ cup (120 ml) water

2 tablespoons (28 ml) cider vinegar

2 medium yellow onions, sliced

1 green bell pepper, cut into thin strips

2 tablespoons (30 g) brown sugar

2 teaspoons kosher salt

2 teaspoons dry mustard

2 teaspoons ground thyme

METHOD

1. Cover the beans with cold water in a bowl and let soak overnight. Or opt for the quick soak: Cover with a couple of inches of water in a good-size pot and bring to a boil for 2 minutes. Remove the pan from the heat, cover, and let the beans soak in the water for 1 hour. Whether you soak the beans overnight or do the quick soak, after they have been soaked, bring the water to a boil and then cook the beans at a simmer for 1 hour. Allow to cool, and then drain the beans and reserve.

2. Preheat your wood-fired oven. When ready to cook the beans, you want the fire to be waning and at about 350°F (180°C).

3. Heat a large Dutch oven in the wood-fired oven for 5 minutes. Remove the Dutch oven and add the vegetable oil. Place the beef roast in the pot and put the pot back in the oven. Allow the roast to brown on all sides, turning as necessary. Add all the remaining ingredients, including the beans, and cover the Dutch oven. Nestle the pot into the ashes of the waning fire in the oven. Cook for 2½ to 3 hours.

4. To serve, cut the beef roast into chunks and serve with a good helping of beans, your favorite hot pepper sauce and, if they're available, a warm biscuit or two.

Serves 4 to 6; makes 3 cups (705 ml) sauce

Cowboy Steak with Whiskey Sauce

I've almost completely stopped serving individual steaks to people, opting instead for large—2- to 3-pound (905 g to 1.4 kg)—steaks for slicing. When placed on a platter, all sliced and perfectly cooked, this allows diners to take the amount their hunger dictates. If, by chance, I bought too big of a steak to begin with, it's great to have those leftover slices the next day for a good-as-it-gets steak sandwich.

Big baked potatoes with all the fixings or a pot of chili beans work as side dishes, as does a crisp salad dressed with a simple vinaigrette. The Whiskey Sauce has enough flavor components going on that you need not provide competition with a complex salad dressing.

INGREDIENTS

(for the steak)

1 sirloin steak, about 3 pounds (1.4 kg), 2 inches (5 cm) thick

1 tablespoon (5 g) black peppercorns, cracked

4 garlic cloves, minced

Olive oil, if needed

(for the whiskey sauce)

1 pound (455 g) unsalted butter

½ cup (80 g) finely chopped onion

2 garlic cloves, minced

½ cup (120 ml) whiskey (your choice)

¼ cup (60 ml) Worcestershire sauce

1 tablespoon (6 g) freshly ground black pepper

1½ teaspoons dry mustard

1 teaspoon salt

Tabasco or other hot pepper sauce

METHOD

1. To make the steak: Trim excess fat from the steak. Pat dry. Press the cracked peppercorns and garlic into both sides of the steak and let stand at room temperature for 1 hour.

2. Preheat your wood-fired oven to between 450°F and 500°F (230°C and 250°C).

3. While the steak is sitting at room temperature, make the sauce: Melt the butter in a saucepan; add the onion and garlic and cook over low heat until the onion is soft. Add all of the remaining ingredients and stir to mix.

4. There are two excellent ways of cooking a steak—any steak—in a wood-fired oven: using a wire cooling rack and pan (see page 69) or using a cast-iron skillet.

If you're using the rack-and-pan method: Place the steak on a wire rack set over a pan. Place the pan next to the fire in the oven. Close the door almost completely and let the steak cook for 15 minutes, at which point the steak will be nicely browned on the outside and rare inside.

If you're using a cast-iron skillet: Rake the hot coals into an even layer and place the skillet directly on top of the coals to preheat. Add a little olive oil to the pan and swirl to coat. Add the steaks and cook for about 2 minutes per side to sear the outside. Move the pan off the coals and set it on the floor of the oven, next to the fire. Allow to cook for another 6 minutes or so, turning if necessary. After 10 minutes or so of total cooking time, start taking the internal temperature, and remove the steak when it is 10°F (5°C) below the temperature you want.

It should be emphasized that the only way to be certain that your steak turns out the way you want is by using an instant-read meat thermometer. No matter what degree of doneness suits you, take the steak out of the oven when its internal temperature has reached 10°F (5°C) shy of where you want it to wind up. For a medium-rare steak, I take my steak out when it reaches 125°F (52°C).

5. With either method of cooking, remove the steak from the oven and loosely tent with aluminum foil for 5 minutes or so. The temperature will continue to climb while the steak is resting. Slice and serve immediately with the sauce.

Serves 14 to 16

Porchetta

Depending on where you're originally from or where you live now, either you'll be familiar with porchetta or it will be completely foreign to you. In essence, it's a boneless, center-cut pork loin completely wrapped in a large piece of pork belly and then roasted. In short, it's what one wag called "pork wrapped in pork." What's not to love?

INGREDIENTS

1 fresh pork belly, 5 to 6 pounds
(2.3 to 2.7 kg), skin on

1 boneless, center-cut pork loin,
3 pounds (1.4 kg)

3 tablespoons (17 g) fennel seeds

1 teaspoon crushed red pepper flakes

2 tablespoons (28 ml) olive oil

1½ tablespoons (3.8 g) chopped fresh
sage leaves

1½ tablespoons (2.5 g) chopped fresh
rosemary leaves

1½ tablespoons (3.6 g) fresh thyme leaves

4 garlic cloves, pressed

Kosher salt and freshly ground black pepper

½ orange, seeded, rind on, cut into very thin slices

METHOD

1. This is a dish that benefits from having a good relationship with your butcher. When you order the fresh pork belly and the center-cut pork loin, it's a good idea to tell your butcher what you're making. He or she will understand that you need the two pieces of pork to "fit"—that is, the loin should be the same length as the width of the pork belly, so when you wrap the belly around the loin, it doesn't overhang the loin at either end. Then test the length of the pork belly by placing it skin-side down and placing the loin in the center of the belly; you want the belly to be just large enough to roll around the entire loin and meet end-to-end, with no overlap. If the belly does overlap, trim with a sharp knife. And for heaven's sake, you don't want the pork belly to be so thick you can't wrap it around the loin. Like I said, a good relationship with your butcher is an important aspect for the successful preparation of this classic dish.

2. Preheat your wood-fired oven to be good and hot: about 500°F (250°C).

3. In a small frying pan over medium heat, warm the fennel seeds and red pepper flakes until lightly toasted, a minute or so. Let cool briefly. Pour the olive oil, cooled fennel seeds and red pepper flakes, sage, rosemary, thyme, and garlic into a small bowl and mix thoroughly using your fingers. Set aside.

4. Place the pork belly skin-side down on a cutting board and, using a sharp knife, score the flesh approximately ⅜ inch (9 mm) deep in a crisscross pattern. Turn the belly over and, using the tip of a sharp knife, make several dozen holes all over the skin, about ⅛ inch (3 mm) deep. Then, using the spiky side of a metal meat mallet, thoroughly pound the skin all over. This will help the skin puff up and crisp when roasted.

5. Turn the belly skin-side down again and dust it and the loin with salt and pepper. Rub the flesh side of the belly and the loin with the reserved olive oil–spice mixture. Put the loin into position on the pork belly and top with overlapping orange slices.

6. Wrap the pork belly around the loin roast and truss with kitchen twine to hold it together.

7. Place the tied roast on a wire rack set on a shallow pan and allow to come to room temperature. Place the pan on the floor of the 500°F (250°C) oven and close the door almost completely. Ideally, after the initial period of high heat (maybe 40 minutes), allow the oven temperature to fall into the 300°F (150°C) range and roast the pork for another 1½ to 2 hours. You may have to add small amounts of smallish firewood to keep the temperature from falling below 300°F (150°C). There's no need to baste the roast; it will be done when the internal temperature reaches 140°F (60°C).

8. Once it has reached temperature, remove it from the oven and loosely tent it with aluminum foil for about 10 minutes. When ready to serve, cut the strings and then, using a large serrated knife, cut into slices or chunks. This is excellent with Slow-Cooked Italian White Beans (page 114).

Serves 2

Country-Style Pork Ribs, Asian Style

Country-style pork ribs aren't really ribs at all—they're substantial strips of pork cut either from the blade end near the shoulder or the shoulder proper. They are offered either boneless or bone-in; I always favor the bone-in version, thinking the bones add flavor (as in "the closer to the bone, the sweeter the meat"). The fat-to-meat ratio is good, making for some very succulent morsels, and you can't beat the price of this cut. I cook up three or four meaty "ribs" at a time and then serve them in all manner of dishes the following week—everything from pork fried rice to chimichangas (what can I say?). The Asian-style marinade makes the pork very versatile and cross-cultural!

INGREDIENTS

½ cup (120 ml) soy sauce

¼ cup (60 ml) sriracha

¼ cup (60 ml) sweet Thai chili sauce

4 country-style pork ribs, bone-in, about 3 pounds (1.4 kg)

METHOD

1. Mix the soy sauce, sriracha, and chili sauce in a 1-gallon (3.8 L) resealable plastic bag. Squish to mix.

2. Add the pork ribs, seal the bag, and allow to marinate in the refrigerator for 1 to 2 hours. This marinade is full-flavored and a longer marinating time is not necessary.

3. Preheat your wood-fired oven. You want the oven temperature to be in the 300°F (150°C) range for cooking, but with enough residual built-up heat for the oven to stay at that temperature for an hour or so.

4. Because of the ratio of meat to fat, low and slow is the way to go with this cut, rendering as much fat as possible while still leaving the ribs very tender. Preheat a Tuscan grill a few inches away from the fire. Once it is hot, remove the ribs from the marinade and place on the Tuscan grill, not touching. Keep the door almost completely closed during cooking.

5. Turn the grill 180 degrees a couple of times while cooking. After about 50 minutes, the ribs will be done (145°F, or 63°C, on an instant-read meat thermometer). Remove from the oven and place on a platter. Loosely tent with aluminum foil for 10 minutes or so. Serve hot or at room temperature.

Serves 10 to 12

Tacos al Pastor

Al pastor means "shepherd style," referring to the fact that this Mexican recipe is based on a Lebanese one featuring lamb. Did you know that the Lebanese started migrating to Mexico in the late nineteenth century? Neither did I, but they brought with them the tradition of grilling slices of lamb stacked on a vertical spit that rotated in front of a live fire. Mexican cooks switched out the lamb for pork and, somewhere along the way, fresh pineapple made its way into the dish. The rest is, as they say, *delicioso.* When I made these recently, one young diner admitted to eating nine of them. Yes, they are that good.

INGREDIENTS

(for the tacos)

10 guajillo chiles, seeded

2 chiles de árbol

2 cups (470 ml) water

1 ripe pineapple

4 to 5 pounds (1.8 to 2.3 kg) boneless pork shoulder (Boston butt), sliced ¾ inch (2 cm) thick

8 garlic cloves, peeled

¾ cup (175 ml) distilled white vinegar

¼ cup (50 g) sugar

¼ cup (76 g) kosher salt

3 tablespoons (48 g) prepared achiote paste

½ medium white onion, cut into chunks

(for the salsa)

2 jalapeño chiles, seeded and diced

½ cup (80 g) finely chopped white onion

½ cup (20 g) chopped fresh mint

½ cup (8 g) chopped fresh cilantro

Juice of 2 fresh limes

Salt

16 corn tortillas

Bottled hot pepper sauce

Lime wedges

METHOD

1. To make the tacos: Bring the guajillo chiles, chiles de árbol, and water to a boil in a medium saucepan over medium-high heat. Cover, remove from the heat, and let sit for 30 minutes to let the chiles soften.

2. Cut the top off the pineapple. Cut off the peel. Cut the remaining pineapple in half lengthwise. Remove and discard the core from both halves. Cut the cored pineapple into chunks, separated into two equal piles.

3. Place the pork in a large bowl. Purée the chiles and their soaking liquid, the garlic, vinegar, sugar, salt, achiote paste, half of the cored pineapple, and the onion chunks in a blender until smooth, about 2 minutes. Pour over the pork, stirring to coat thoroughly. Cover and marinate in the refrigerator for 3 to 12 hours.

4. When ready to cook, preheat your wood-fired oven to between 450°F and 500°F (230°C and 250°C).

5. Add the marinated pork slices to a lightly greased pan (preferably cast-iron) or on a wire cooking rack set into pan.

6. Place the pan with the pork in the oven, next to the embers. Turn the pan 90 degrees every 10 minutes or so to cook evenly. Start checking for doneness after 30 minutes with an instant-read thermometer. Once the pork reaches 145°F (63 °C) (which the USDA now considers safe for pork) remove from the oven, tent loosely with aluminum foil, and let rest for 10 minutes.

Serves 6 to 8

Leg of Lamb

When I was growing up, Sunday night dinners often featured roast leg of lamb—cooked well-done and served with that bright green mint jelly. Given that, it's amazing I'm including a recipe for leg of lamb here, but, thankfully, somewhere along the way I was introduced to medium-rare lamb flavored with garlic and rosemary. Embracing this discovery almost got me banished from my family, but some things are worth it. Serve with Roasted Vegetable Medley (page 94) or Slow-Cooked Italian White Beans (page 114). Leave the mint jelly on the shelf at the grocery store.

INGREDIENTS

1 leg of lamb, 6 to 7 pounds (2.7 to 3.2 kg), bone-in

10 or 12 small fresh rosemary sprigs, about ½ inch (1.2 cm) long

5 or 6 garlic cloves, sliced in half

⅓ cup (80 ml) extra-virgin olive oil

Kosher salt and freshly ground black pepper

METHOD

1. Preheat your wood-fired oven to be a medium-high heat, about 400°F (200°C).

2. Using the tip of a very sharp knife, make 10 to 12 incisions all over the top and sides of the lamb roast. Push a sprig of rosemary and one-half garlic clove into each incision. Rub the olive oil all over the roast and dust with salt and pepper.

3. Place the lamb on a wire rack set in a roasting pan. Allow to come to room temperature.

4. Put the lamb in the oven, close the door almost all the way, and roast until the lamb reaches 130°F to 135°F (54°C to 57°C), about 1½ hours for medium-rare.

5. Remove the lamb from the oven, tent loosely with aluminum foil, and allow to rest for 10 minutes before carving so the juices will redistribute. Carve against the grain using the bone as a handle.

Serves 4 to 6

Roasted Vegetable Medley

Notice I didn't call this ratatouille (which is its own distinct dish) or vegetable stew (which just doesn't sound all that appealing). Sometime over the last generation or so, the classic ratatouille (which is a combination of onion, tomato, eggplant, and zucchini) morphed into a more free-form dish composed of cooked summer vegetables, often including bell peppers and fennel. I say let's call it a medley and include anything that appeals to you from the following list, leaving out the vegetables you don't like. Or, for a beautiful and delicious variation, choose the vegetables on the basis of their colors, such as yellow crookneck squash, yellow and gold tomatoes, and yellow or orange peppers, and produce a dish with all the colors of sunshine.

INGREDIENTS

2 to 3 pounds (0.9-1.4 kg) of cut vegetables, including:

- Eggplant, including the long, skinny Japanese eggplant
- All kinds of tomatoes
- All kinds of peppers
- All kinds of summer squash
- Onions

Garlic

Fennel

Olive oil

Capers

Basil

Oregano

Salt and freshly ground black pepper

METHOD

1. Preheat your wood-fired oven to about 400°F (200°C).

2. Cut up the vegetables into approximately 1-inch (2.5 cm) pieces.

3. Add enough olive oil to an earthenware casserole or stainless-steel pan to generously coat it. Add the vegetables, capers, and herbs, along with salt and freshly ground pepper, and toss the vegetables until they are all coated with the oil and seasonings. You can cover the pan or casserole if you want the vegetables evenly steamed or leave it uncovered for a more rustic, slightly smoky taste with a few charred edges here and there. Bake in the oven until cooked to your desired degree of doneness, testing after about 15 minutes.

4. You can serve the medley as is or dress the dish with chopped fresh herbs and a little more olive oil and a splash of vinegar. Serve warm or at room temperature.

Serves 4

Smashed New Potatoes with Miso Mayonnaise

Be forewarned: there's an addictive quality to these potatoes that goes beyond their simple ingredients. Originally inspired by a recipe I ran across on the website Food52, I made some changes and can tell you that it is some kind of wonderful. It's best served hot out of the oven.

INGREDIENTS

1½ pounds (680 g) small new potatoes, about the size of golf balls

Olive oil

½ cup (115 g) mayonnaise

1 tablespoon (16 g) miso paste, brown preferred

Zest and juice of 1 lemon

2 or 3 scallions, thinly sliced, for garnish

METHOD

1. Preheat your wood-fired oven to about 500°F (250°C).

2. Steam the potatoes in a covered pan until the tip of a sharp knife pierces the flesh to the middle easily.

3. Choose a baking pan that will fit the potatoes in a single layer. Coat the pan liberally with olive oil. Once the potatoes have cooled enough to handle, place them one at a time in the pan and gently flatten with the heel of your hand. Be careful not to smash the potatoes apart. Turn the flattened potatoes carefully so that both sides are coated with oil. Place the pan in the oven.

4. Make the mayonnaise sauce by combining the mayonnaise, miso, lemon zest, and lemon juice in a bowl using a fork.

5. Once the potatoes have formed a golden crust on one side—after 10 minutes or so—flip them and allow them to crisp on the other side. Once they are done, the potatoes can be served right from the pan, topped with the mayonnaise sauce and a scattering of the sliced scallions. Enjoy!

Roasted Tomatoes

These are the essence of simplicity and a definite crowd-pleaser. A cupcake pan is the perfect cooking pan; if you don't have one, you can fashion a facsimile by scrunching aluminum foil into a shape that holds individual tomatoes upright. For the record, even relatively hard, out-of-season tomatoes are transformed by the wood-fired heat into a very tasty side dish.

INGREDIENTS

(per person)

1 tomato

½ teaspoon olive oil

1 teaspoon prepared pesto

Salt and freshly ground black pepper

1 tablespoon (5 g) grated Parmesan cheese

METHOD

1. Preheat your wood-fired oven to about 450°F (230°C).

2. Slice the top one-quarter (or less) from each tomato. Using the tip of a sharp, serrated knife, remove almost all of the core of the tomato, leaving the last bit at the bottom to act as a "plug" to keep the pesto from draining out.

3. Drizzle each tomato with the olive oil, fill the void with the pesto, and sprinkle the top with salt and pepper.

4. Sprinkle the top of each tomato with the Parmesan. Place the tomatoes in the cupcake pan or makeshift aluminum foil pan.

5. The tomatoes will heat through in about 15 minutes. Serve hot or at room temperature.

Go-To Mixed Greens

All kinds of greens—from spinach to Swiss chard to all types of mustard greens and kales—are a great, fast-cooking addition to wood-fired fare, especially good for folks wanting to avoid carbohydrates. Anyone familiar with cooking fresh greens by more traditional methods knows that a mountain of greens quickly cooks down to just a couple of individual servings. Because of this, my favored cooking container for greens is one of those large disposable aluminum roasting pans (like the ones used to cook turkeys), only I don't consider them "disposable." The procedure outlined below is based on individual heads of greens as they are sold at grocery stores. I wish I could say that each head will serve two people, but it all depends on how generous the heads are and how much you and your diners like greens. I'd say play it safe and count on one-and-a-half heads per person, which, just so you know, is going to look like a lot of fresh greens.

INGREDIENTS

(per person)

2 tablespoons (28 ml) olive oil

1½ heads greens

1 tablespoon (15 ml) vinegar, preferably sherry vinegar

Garlic cloves, pressed, as desired

Salt and freshly ground black pepper

METHOD

1. Preheat your wood-fired oven to about 450°F (230°C).

2. Add the olive oil to the roasting pan and, using your fingers, rub the oil over the bottom and sides of the pan.

3. Coarsely chop the greens and add them to the pan. Sprinkle with the vinegar and add the garlic and salt and pepper. Mix to coat the greens, and place them in the oven. The greens will cook so quickly that there's no real need to cover them. Toss them every couple of minutes just until they have turned bright green and wilted. Serve immediately, with an additional dressing of oil and vinegar, if desired.

Serves 6

Break-the-Rules Risotto

A fair amount of mystique surrounds the traditional making of risotto, most of which has to do with gentle and consistent stirring over a long period of time. Frankly, I had my doubts about cooking it in a wood-fired oven because there was no way I could give it the kind of attention in the stirring department as I was supposedly supposed to. I decided to give it a try anyway and made it in my earthenware bean pot because it seemed about the right size and I knew it could withstand the high heat of the oven. Like I said, gentle, regular stirring was out of the question, and I'm sure the temperature was much higher than anyone would ever recommend, so I basically broke every rule for making risotto, and you know what? It turned out perfectly. I'm sure there's a lesson in there—I just haven't figured out what it is yet.

INGREDIENTS

4 tablespoons (55 g) unsalted butter

1 tablespoon (15 ml) olive oil

½ medium yellow onion, finely chopped

5 cups (1.2 L) chicken or vegetable broth

1 cup (235 ml) dry white wine

2 cups (390 g) Arborio rice

1 cup (100 g) grated Parmesan cheese

Salt and freshly cracked black or white pepper

METHOD

1. Preheat your wood-fired oven to about 400°F (200°C).

2. Put 2 tablespoons (27.5 g) of the butter and the olive oil in the bean pot and place in the oven to melt. Add the onion, stir, and place back in the oven for 10 minutes or so, just long enough to soften the onion.

3. Combine the broth and wine in a large pitcher.

4. Add the rice to the sautéed onion and stir to coat the rice in the oil and butter. Add 4½ cups (1070 ml) of the broth to the pot and stir; reserve the leftover wine and broth combination. Cover the pot with its lid and place in the oven. If you have a live fire in the cooking chamber, turn the pot 90 degrees every 15 minutes.

5. Check the rice after 1 hour or so. Most likely it will have absorbed all the liquid. If so, add about ½ cup (120 ml) of the reserved wine and broth combination, the Parmesan, and the remaining 2 tablespoons (27.5 g) butter and stir to incorporate. Replace the lid and put the pot back in a cooler part of the oven until you're ready to serve. If, when you check the rice after an hour of cooking, it's still not done, stir in ½ cup (120 ml) of the wine and broth combination, cover the pot, and place back in the oven for an additional 10 to 15 minutes before adding more broth, the Parmesan, and the remaining butter.

Makes about 7 cups (1.6 L)

Slow-Cooked Italian White Beans

The Italian tradition of cooking white beans overnight in a Chianti bottle (cannellini in fiasco) nestled into the ashes of a still-hot wood-fired oven has always appealed to me. Although, if I'm honest, it seems kind of silly to shake the beans out of the bottle, more or less one at a time, once they're cooked. And I've always been a little spooked about the possibility of the Chianti bottle breaking if the heat accidentally got too high. These beans are so good, I'd hate to waste them. Truth be told, most folks (even in Italy) have stopped using an empty Chianti bottle and now favor a glazed earthenware bean pot (called a *coccio*) with a lid. Makes sense to me.

INGREDIENTS

1 pound (455 g) dried cannellini beans, rinsed and picked over

¼ cup (60 ml) good-quality olive oil (the greener and fruitier, the better)

½ medium yellow onion, diced

4 medium fresh sage leaves

8 medium garlic cloves, quartered

¼ teaspoon crushed red pepper flakes

Kosher salt and freshly ground black pepper

(special equipment)

An 8-quart (7.5 L) heat-proof glazed terra-cotta bean pot with a lid

METHOD

1. There are two ways to cook the cannellini beans: fast or slow. If you decide to cook them fast (in an hour or less), you'll need to either soak the beans overnight or do a fast soak: put the beans in a good-size pot and cover with a couple of inches of water. Bring the water to a boil over high heat. Cook the beans for 2 minutes. Remove the pan from the heat, cover, and let the beans soak in the water for 1 hour. Drain and proceed with the recipe.

   If you decide on the slow method, there's no need to presoak or fast-soak the beans. Just proceed with the recipe and count on between 3 and 4 hours (or overnight) for the beans to cook.

2. Preheat your wood-fired oven. You want to cook the beans in the ashes of a waning fire, at about 350°F (180°C).

3. Mix the beans with the olive oil, onion, sage, garlic, red pepper flakes, and salt and pepper in the bean pot.

4. Cover the beans with water; cover the bean pot and nestle it into the ashes of the waning fire. If you've presoaked the beans, they should be ready in an hour or so, although older beans take longer to cook than a new crop, so be prepared. If you haven't soaked the beans, do like the Italians do: just put them in the dying fire and go to bed. They'll be ready to use the following morning—in soups and stews, as a side dish (especially wonderful with roast lamb), or as a white bean dip on bruschetta.

Makes about 8 cups (1.9 L)

Cowboy Chili Beans

Every good home cook needs a couple of tricks up his or her sleeve, and this is one of them: four ingredients that produce flavorful and versatile beans. If you're not familiar with Ro-Tel, you need to be: it's a quality product, finally with the nationwide distribution it deserves. It's worth splurging on an earthenware bean pot for this recipe alone.

INGREDIENTS

1 pound (455 g) dried pinto beans, rinsed and picked over

2 cans (10 ounces, or 280 g) Ro-Tel (diced tomatoes with green chiles)

1 tablespoon (7.5 g) chili powder

1 teaspoon ground cumin

(special equipment)

An 8-quart (7.5 L) heat-proof glazed terra-cotta bean pot with a lid

METHOD

1. To start, you'll need to either soak the beans over night or do a fast soak. For a fast soak, put the beans in a good-size pot and cover with a couple of inches of water. Bring the water to a boil over high heat. Cook the beans for 2 minutes. Remove the pan from the heat, cover, and let the beans soak in the water for 1 hour. For the overnight soak, simply put the beans in a large pot, add enough water to cover the beans by a couple of inches, and let sit overnight. Once they've been soaked, whether fast or overnight, drain them and proceed with the recipe.

2. Preheat your wood-fired oven to between 350°F and 400°F (180°C and 200°C).

3. Mix the beans with the Ro-Tel, the chili powder, and the cumin in the bean pot. Add water to cover the beans by about 1 inch (2.5 cm).

4. Cover the bean pot and nestle it into the ashes of the waning fire. The beans should be ready in 1 hour to 1 hour 30 minutes, although older beans take longer to cook than a new crop, so be prepared. If you haven't presoaked the beans, do like the Italians do: just put them in your bean pot, nestle the pot in the dying fire, and go to bed. They'll be ready to use the following morning.

Sources

Wood-fired ovens come in a variety of forms—fully manufactured; as kits to assemble; and as custom installations created by a contractor. They are sold in home-supply centers, garden centers, and patio/hearth stores, but they are not as widely available as, say, grills or smokers. Sometimes you will need to contact the manufacturer either to order directly or to find a local retailer. The following are the more prominent manufacturers.

Californo
209 NW 4th Avenue
Hallandale Beach FL 33009
855-553-6766
www.californo.co

Oven kits and accessories.

Camp Chef
3985 N 75 W
Hyde Park, UT 84318
800-650-2433
www.campchef.com

Ovens and accessories.

Forno Piombo
728 1st Street
Napa, CA 94559
707-287-6931
www.fornopiombo.com

Sells ovens and offers cooking classes.

Green Mountain Grills

316 California Avenue, Suite 1065
Reno, NV 89509
800-603-3398
www.greenmountaingrills.com

Sells wood-burning-oven converter boxes for
its range of pellet grills and smokers.

ilFornino

711 Executive Boulevard, Suite U
Valley Cottage, NY 10989
877-302-6660
www.ilfornino.com

Ovens and accessories.

PizzaQue

The Companion Group
1250 9th Street
Berkeley, CA 94710
866-682-2060
www.pizzacraft.com

Ovens and accessories.

Roccbox

www.roccbox.com

Headquartered in England, but sells a hybrid gas
and wood-burning outdoor oven in North
America as well.

Uuni North America

www.uuni.net

Headquartered in Scotland, but sells ovens and
accessories in North America as well.

Acknowledgments

Thanks to the Behrens clan of Behrens Family Winery in the hills above St. Helena for being willing participants in this venture, not to mention such good eaters, and for their magnificent al fresco kitchen.

Thanks also to the folks at Shackford's Kitchen Store—Napa's home-grown source for all things culinary—for being enthusiastic neighbors and generous providers of props and hard-to-find supplies.

And thank you Tony Piombo of Forno Piombo (www.fornopiombo.com) for letting me use your beautiful, hand-crafted wood-fired ovens in that great setting overlooking the Napa River.

About the Author

A. Cort Sinnes is an award-winning author of more than thirty-six books on cooking and gardening including *The Grilling Book*, *The New Gas Grill Gourmet*, and *The Grilling Encyclopedia*, which was nominated for a James Beard Award. He is a lifelong resident of California's Napa Valley.

Index